The Ch
and
Freemasonry

Published on behalf of
The Panel on Doctrine
of The Church of Scotland
by The Saint Andrew Press,
121 George Street, Edinburgh EH2 4YN

First published in 1990 by The Saint Andrew Press on behalf of
The Panel on Doctrine of the Church of Scotland,
121 George Street, Edinburgh EH2 4YN

Copyright © 1990 The Panel on Doctrine of the Church of Scotland

ISBN: 0 86153 115 9

This booklet is set in 11/12pt Times.

Typeset and printed by Hugh K. Clarkson & Sons Ltd., Young Street, West Calder, West Lothian EH55 8EQ.

T HE Report of the Panel on Doctrine on the Church and Freemasonry was approved by the General Assembly of the Church of Scotland in 1989. It is important that its contents be made as widely available as possible since the Assembly also encouraged members of the Church of Scotland who are involved in Freemasonry "to reconsider their involvement in the light of the Report".

The Panel on Doctrine was not asked to carry out a full investigation of Freemasonry in all its aspects. Such a task would have been beyond our scope as a Panel. Our study was primarily concerned with the relationship between the Craft and Christianity. And we did not seek to address Freemasonry as such, but those members of the Kirk who are also freemasons. As a Panel on Doctrine we wished to show pastoral concern and to share the difficulties we have. We have sought to be positive rather than negative, setting forth the truths of the gospel of God's grace in Jesus Christ our Lord.

We have not used the language of compatibility and incompatibility. We feel there should be no question about the prior claims of the gospel and the Church and Christians over all other claims. What we do think is that such practices are unworthy of those whose first allegiance must be to Christ.

In the light of our report, church members involved in Freemasonry are being asked by the General Assembly to think again. We consider that such is an appropriate response and in line with our nature as a reformed church in that we leave such matters to the conscience of the individual. We do not think the Church should be seeking to excommunicate or carry out heresy hunts. We do think the Church should offer guidance to those who are concerned or puzzled about the relationship between Freemasonry and Christianity.

Douglas M. Murray
Convener of the Panel on Doctrine

THE CHURCH AND FREEMASONRY

T HE General Assembly of The Church of Scotland in 1987 accepted an Overture from the Presbytery of Aberdeen pointing out that other Christian churches had affirmed the incompatibility of Christianity and Freemasonry and instructing the Panel on Doctrine "to examine the theological issues involved in Church members being also Freemasons; to consider the compatibility or otherwise of Freemasonry with Christianity; and in particular to determine whether the rituals and the teachings of Freemasonry are consistent with the Church of Scotland's belief in the gospel of the sovereign grace and love of God, wherein through Jesus Christ, his only Son, our Lord, Incarnate, Crucified and Risen, he freely offers to all men, upon repentance and faith, the forgiveness of sins, renewal by the Holy Spirit, and eternal life".

As a supplementary deliverance to that, whereby the General Assembly agreed to transmit this Overture to the Panel on Doctrine, the Panel was instructed to consult with the Grand Lodge of Scotland during the course of its deliberations.

The Panel on Doctrine established a Working Party under the convenership of the Reverend Dr A. Stewart Todd. The membership of the Working Party comprised the Reverend A.H. Symington (Secretary), the Reverend Dr D.M. Murray, the Reverend D.M. Beckett, the Reverend Professor R. Davidson, the Reverend C.R. Williamson and Miss E. Scott.

The Working Party has met regularly over two years, and as the Assembly will recognise has been involved in an immense task of seeking, sifting and studying information at its disposal. It is grateful to all those who wrote offering many insights based on personal experience, and in particular to ministers and members of the Church who voluntarily presented submissions for study. It is also grateful to every church tradition in Scotland and beyond, to which it wrote, for

1

the courteous response it received, and for the help advanced.

Much reading was done, and although the Working Party recognises that the traditions of English Freemasonry are not altogether the same as those of Scottish Freemasonry, nonetheless it found the reports both to the Church of England General Synod and to the Methodist Conference of great help. Perhaps it is this difference of masonic tradition that precluded the Grand Lodge in Scotland from being able to offer the Working Party any specific reasons as to where these reports were misguided, or simply wrong.

After a period of study and of sharing the fruits of that study, the Working Party communicated with the Grand Lodge of Scotland, and acknowledges the positive approach that came from the office-bearers. Particular thanks should be extended to Mr Arthur Hazel, the Grand Secretary of the Grand Lodge of Scotland of Ancient, Free and Accepted Masons. A certain amount of reading material was presented to the Working Party directly from Grand Lodge, and in the light of the submissions and other material, a list of questions was prepared by the Working Party, and sent to the Grand Lodge for the Working Party's clarification, and also to form the basis of questioning that members of the Working Party conducted in meeting with the Grand Lodge. The frank answering of these questions was much appreciated and, in particular, the positive statements made in them concerning the position of Freemasonry *vis-à-vis* the role and status of parish ministers. The advice in the Report which is directed towards ministers comes from these statements.

In September 1988, the Working Party, feeling that sufficient preparatory steps had been taken to render a meeting with Grand Lodge meaningful, accepted an invitation to attend a meeting at Freemasons' Hall, Edinburgh. The members were warmly received by J.M. Marcus Humphrey of Dinnet, Grand Master Mason, the Right Honourable the Earl of Elgin and Kincardine, past Grand Master, the Reverend Ian Macdonald, senior Grand Chaplain, the Reverend Joseph J. Morrow, Junior Grand Chaplain, nine other named representatives, and some other unnamed representatives. The meeting was very helpful, and the Working Party welcomed the advice which it had already sought to act upon, to contact other branches of

Freemasonry, including those which have specific Christian connotations. In that respect, further meetings were held with the Supreme Grand Royal Arch Chapter of Scotland, and with the Supreme Council for Scotland of the Thirty-third Degree of the Ancient and Accepted Scottish Rite. In these meetings too, the Working Party acknowledges the willingness of the representatives of Freemasonry to enter into discussion, and thanks all those who contributed to its wider understanding.

It must be emphasised that the Panel's Working Party sought at all times to derive as much information from members of Grand Lodge as possible, and also to recognise that in Freemasonry there are many valued members and ministers of the Church. The remit, however, was clearly before the Working Party in terms of theological and doctrinal emphasis, and in the Report it is faithfulness to that remit which the Working Party attempts to honour.

We did, however, feel that since we were considering specifically the position of fellow-Christians within Freemasonry our Report, as well as being analytical, should also exhibit pastoral concern and we therefore decided to express that concern by casting the bulk of our material in the form of a letter.

A Letter to Members of the Church of Scotland within Freemasonry

We on the Panel write this letter to you as to friends, as to fellow members of the body of Christ. We write with great earnestness. We shall endeavour to express ourselves with clarity. We are led by your spokesmen to believe that you are numerous and that you are likely to be bewildered and hurt if we make any adverse comment on Freemasonry. We should like to make it clear to you that our concern as a Panel on Doctrine has not been to carry out an investigation of all aspects of Freemasonry in Scotland, or to pass judgement on the moral character of its members. The submission which came with the Overture to the Assembly from the Presbytery of Aberdeen spoke of the fine people who are involved in Freemasonry, including many Church members, and of the work they do in caring for others and supporting charitable causes. In our meetings with representatives of the Grand Lodge of Scotland and the Supreme Grand Royal Arch Chapter of Scotland we were made aware of the ways in which you helped not only your own members but the wider community of which you are part. We are not concerned to criticise the conduct of Freemasons: on the contrary we commend your charitable work. We do, however, have very real theological difficulties.

You have told us in your reply to our queries that Freemasonry "although of a religious character, is not itself a religion": you may think therefore that there is no theology in Freemasonry itself and that any theology there is is the input of the individual person, in your case Christian, in others the input of another faith. When pressed further one of your spokesmen compared Freemasonry to the Scout movement. But you have a chaplain and he says prayers and we are able to read your prayers for they are available in print, and in your prayers you address God and you give him titles: "Almighty Father" and "Supreme Ruler of the Universe". You speak of his "honour" and "glory" and of his "Holy Name". You attribute to him "Divine Wisdom" and you speak of his "aid" and his "enabling" a candidate "assisted by the secrets" of Freemasonry, the better to display the "beauties of true godliness" (*The Standard Ritual of Scottish Freemasonry*, p.7).

Then you have a theology: these words that you use in your prayer constitute in themselves a theology – a knowledge of God. They are not vacuous words, empty of meaning until you make your mental Christian input or the Muslim makes his mental Muslim input. Not at all! They are a neat compilation of intelligent and consequential ideas. Complemented as they are by your exhortations and by what you describe as your "charades" your prayers are all too clear: our complaint is not just that the name of Jesus is suppressed in them, our complaint is also that he doesn't seem to be required! To what purpose was his life and victorious death, to what end his resurrection and exaltation and his return in the power of the Holy Spirit if the Supreme Being (who can be not the Christian God but the God of some other faith) in co-operation with Freemasonry can enable a man to display the beauties of true godliness? Beloved in Christ this is unworthy of you. This is deism: it had a vogue two centuries ago: it is long since discredited in Christian circles. Of course we should chide other Christians who fall into the same

4

theological trap sometimes but they don't always write and publish prayers!

It is argued that many fine Christian men are also freemasons. This we would not seek to deny and would be happy to confirm. We were received with courtesy by your representatives, many of whom are ministers and elders of the Kirk. Likewise all of us on the Panel know of faithful Church members and elders who are also freemasons. Again we are not concerned with making judgements on the moral worth of particular freemasons. We are solely concerned with doctrinal matters and with how the teachings of Freemasonry relate to the Christian faith. We want to be positive rather than negative, to set forth the great truths of the gospel and then to ask you to assess your Freemasonry in the light of the grace and love of God in Jesus Christ our Lord.

We refer therefore to the Bible. As you well know the Church of Scotland "acknowledges the word of God, which is contained in the scriptures of the Old and New Testaments, to be the supreme rule of faith and life" (*The Book of Common Order [1979]*, p. 121). It follows that doctrinal matters can never be determined by an appeal to an individual's moral worth or Christian profession. That someone whom we respect and admire holds certain views – for example those of Freemasonry – does not mean that these beliefs must for that reason be true or worthwhile. They must be examined and assessed on different grounds altogether, to see whether or not they are consistent with the word of God as contained in the scriptures. Any other way of dealing with doctrinal matters would be inconsistent with our nature as a Reformed Church.

Of course we commend your concern for moral values and your zeal in inculcating them in your brethren and companions in lodge and chapter. Of course your prayers and homilies demonstrate the seriousness of your intent. Nevertheless we cannot but be disturbed by a system of morality which claims to have validity *for Christians* apart from the Gospel of Christ. Freemasonry is defined as "a system of morality, veiled in allegory and illustrated by symbols" (*The Applicant*, p. 1). Freemasonry claims to assist you to lead the moral life: that is its *raison d'être*. Yet the name of Christ is not mentioned in your rituals and teachings since masons are required to believe only in "the Supreme Being". Men of other religions who believe in God can also be admitted. Indeed you indicate that the morality taught by your organisation is no different from the morality known by people in general. Your representatives explained it like this: "the system of morality to be found in Freemasonry does not add in any way to the knowledge of how the public at large should live, what is written in our rituals is simply on paper what must be in the heart and mind of any mature adult who tries to regulate his life to a high moral standard". And the same point is made in *The Applicant*: "the system of morality to which we have referred as Freemasonry is that which every Freemason is bound to profess and practise. If it includes principles with which he was familiar before his entrance into Freemasonry, he will nevertheless find these presented in new ways and in forms different from those with which he was previously familiar. If he finds in Masonic teachings nothing startingly new, he must remember that, in some respects at least, there is 'nothing new under the sun' and that the essence of morality is to be found in the utter simplicity (though not the ease) of its requirements" (p. 1). Yet in answer to one of our questions one of your spokesmen has said: "the Bible plays a most important role in Freemasonry: it is the basis of our teachings". Then we have to say to you that any system of morality claiming to be Bible-based but shunning all mention of Christ is bound to be, for the Christian, seriously deficient. The Bible witnesses above all to Jesus Christ our Lord, the unique revelation of God, in whom alone we can share in the life which is acceptable to God.

How can you suppress the name of Jesus Christ when the most distinctive feature of Christianity is that it is good news that deserves to be published abroad, good news that cannot and must not be kept silent? The good news is that with Jesus Christ in his life a man shall be able to grow up into moral and spiritual maturity; the good news is that with Christ in our societies the world can inch its way forward towards something more like God's kingdom; the good news is that the beauty of true godliness which you earnestly seek has been seen incomparably in Jesus Christ, in the nobilities of his heart, which nobilities are in the gift of his Holy Spirit to be shared by all who will receive him. Fellow Christians, it is unworthy of you to suppress this gospel. It is unworthy of you to be so selective in your use of the Bible.

We have read your history. We have some impression of your traditions and how they arose. We are intrigued by the craft background and by the links which you claim to have with important events in Scottish history. We admire the quality of your fellowship and the loyalty you can command. We note that it is exported to all parts of the world. We know your charitable works. None of these things justifies what we see as deviation from the mainstream of Christian doctrine as held by our own Church and by the world Church.

Since last we met with you there has appeared a book entitled *The First Freemasons*: the subtitle is "Scotland's Early Lodges and Their Members"; the author is David Stevenson. In that book he writes on p. 10: "Scotland's early Freemasons, it would appear, probably kept specifically religious practices out of their lodges . . . ." If that is true then we can understand perhaps why the Church in those days did not feel it had to write to freemasons such a letter as we are writing now. If you merely presented homiletic material on moral questions in a colourful and dramatic way we could scarcely complain. But you pray! Your thoughts on morality are gathered up in prayer to God and in your words of prayer, from which we quoted above, you endeavour to hallow his name and you speak of his honour and glory. This is surely a specifically religious practice.

Now Christians may on occasion address prayers to Jesus Christ or they may address prayers to the Holy Spirit but the normal Christian prayer is prayer addressed to God the Father, a specific God, Creator, God of Abraham, Isaac and Jacob, the Father of our Lord Jesus Christ, not an abstraction of whatever "Supreme Being" conjures up in the mind of each worshipper. Such prayer is addressed to God "through Jesus Christ our Lord". That phrase is no throw-away, liturgical jingle. It goes to the heart of our Christian understanding of worship and specifically of prayer. Let us just stay with the idea of hallowing God's name. It is a phrase that is very familiar to us from the Lord's Prayer. But let us ask a radical question: "Who hallows God's name?" Presumably only God can hallow his name. You and we are as inadequate for the task of hallowing God's name as we are for the task of causing God's kingdom to come or of ensuring that his will is done. In Ezekiel God promises that he will "sanctify his great name" (36:23). In John's gospel Jesus prays, "Father glorify thy name" – sanctifying the name of God, glorifying it and hallowing it are synonymous – and the answering voice from heaven replies, "I have glorified it, and I will glorify it again" (12:28f). The hallowing of God's name is pre-eminently God's action and we do it in response to God's action. Jesus is the one man who can truly hallow God's name (and Jesus is the Son of God), in the same way as Jesus is the one man in and with whom the kingdom of God has come, and in and by whom alone the will of God is perfectly done. Therefore all our worship is through Jesus Christ our Lord, he being the one true worshipper, he being the risen and exalted one, a man at the right hand of God, making intercession for us. It is in Jesus Christ that we have "boldness and access" (Ephesians 3:2). It is because we have in Jesus Christ a "great high priest that has passed into the heavens" that we may "come boldly unto the throne of grace, that we may obtain mercy, and find grace . . ." (Hebrews 4:14, 16). Again we appeal to you to consider: is it not unworthy of you to spurn this mediation and pass by the true high priest?

Other Christian churches have been worried about the element of secrecy in your organisation: you tell us that the emphasis is not so much on secrecy as on privacy. We see no reason why we should not respect your privacy. If indeed there are no significant secrets now in Freemasonry either for your brothers and companions, for your candidates or for us your friends, then the secrecy motif which still features in some of your rites must be mainly symbolic. It would symbolise, we may suppose, the degree of seriousness with which you regard the subject of the so-called secret. Then we must tell you that in our opinion it is a wholly inappropriate symbol. If Jesus Christ is the Word and the Wisdom of God and the light of the world then you don't hide the light. And if you think there is some other, more profound wisdom somewhere available, then we must label you gnostics and remind you that whenever in history gnosticism has reared its head the Church has always denounced it.

The name gnosticism is derived from the Greek word *gnosis*, meaning knowledge: it is a name given to a complex religious movement which in its Christian form dates from the second century. At the heart of gnosticism there was usually belief in a special knowledge handed down by a secret tradition from an ancient source. The systems of

8

teaching range from genuine speculation to wild amalgams of mythology and magic with only a minimal admixture of Christianity.

Your spokesmen have said you would be bewildered by criticism from the Church. We find ourselves equally bewildered by your reticence about Our Lord, as we have said. Your spokesmen offered some justification for this by saying that limitation to belief in a Supreme Being permits inter-faith contacts. Now it might be right for a Christian in certain circumstances to be party to the use of some minimalist formula and attendant devotions, as a preliminary to a subsequent witness to Christ and to God's almighty act of salvation through Christ, salvation of all men and of their world and of their universe. In inter-faith dialogue it is important that the participants be open and frank about their different perspectives and beliefs and that these differences should not be ignored and suppressed. But this stage cannot be reached in Freemasonry because discussion of religion in your gatherings, we understand, is not permitted! Then you seem to suggest that your "brotherhood" and "companionship" extended to those of other faiths are more promising things than Christianity, for the sake of which greater good, on the subject of Christ the Lord, the light of the world and the light of men, you will be silent. Certainly as the Church we have fragmented the brotherhood we have in Christ most lamentably and the quality of fellowship we display to those of other faiths is very poor, but we do not believe that there is any foundation for the brotherhood of man other than the one that is laid – Jesus Christ. Not to confess Christ before men is again unworthy of you as Christians.

In the light of the foregoing we invite you to reconsider your involvement in Freemasonry.

APPENDIX I

"CHRISTIAN" ORDERS OF FREEMASONRY

The Working Party in its discussions with Grand Lodge, when questioning the absence of any Christian content in the working of craft masonry, was referred to degrees within the masonic system which are avowedly Christian. A Grand Chaplain expressed the opinion that craft masonry was like an open door which invited members to progress further into the Christian degrees.

A meeting was arranged with representatives of the Supreme Council for Scotland of the Thirty-third Degree of the Ancient and Accepted Scottish Rite.

The origins of this working are to be found in eighteenth-century France. After its repression there, it was preserved in the United States. The Council members claimed that Scottish Rite masonry is a system of Christian morality as distinct from the universal morality offered by the Grand Lodge.

The Working Party studied the booklets *The Eighteenth Degree – An Exegesis* and *The Thirtieth Degree – An Exegesis* which explained in general terms the purpose and meaning of the working of the A. & A.S.R. The following paragraphs include quotations from these exegeses.

The degrees following on from craft masonry take the candidate through the exile and restoration of the Jews to the completion of the second Temple. The seventeenth degree "is concerned with the dawn of the Christian era, and, after destruction by the Romans of the second Temple, with the promise of the Spiritual Temple of Universal Humanity designed by 'The Master', and it inculcates a symbolism based on the apocalyptic vision of St John. In it the Candidate, who is an oriental pilgrim, seeks the Perfect Light, and is baptised by fire and water before breaking the seals of the Book of Life and placing it on the emblems of the Craft" (*Eighteenth Degree*, p. 3).

"The symbolism of the eighteenth degree begins with the destruction of this Spiritual Temple when the Headstone of the Corner had been rudely torn from the foundations of the Temple and thrown among its ruins, and the Mystic Rose of Sharon had been nailed to a Cross. In the words of the lecture the Candidate, who is descended from the Princes and Rulers in Israel, finds that 'in an instant human masonry was destroyed, the Veil of the Temple was rent in twain, darkness covered the earth, the Blazing Star disappeared and the Word was lost'" (*Eighteenth Degree*, p. 3).

In the course of the degree working "the Candidate is now led by the three theological virtues (Faith, Hope and Charity) to the Calvary Chamber and his own symbolic death to be re-born, with the assistance of the Word, from death-in-sin to eternal life. Still veiled and carrying the embodiment of the three virtues, the Candidate now goes on a triumphal journey. In the gloriously lighted Chapter Room he has revealed to him that through these virtues he may come closer to God and the Word and the veil is stripped from his eyes" (*Eighteenth Degree*, p. 5).

In this degree the candidate is promoted from speculative masonry to become a Ne Plus Ultra Mason of Heredom, a Knight of the Eagle and Pelican and a Sovereign Prince Rose Croix. The ceremony concludes with a symbolic meal which, the booklet is at pains to point out, is an AGAPE and not a EUCHARIST.

Preparation for the thirtieth degree includes "reflection" during which the candidate "is taught the need for courage and resolution to overcome the changing fortunes of life, and in particular to overcome the fear of death". To that end the principles of a "philosopher" are committed to him. The list of these principles, "magnanimity, moral rectitude, resignation in adversity", etc., includes only one oblique reference to God, *viz*.: "To adore and worship the Supreme Being". Nevertheless they are claimed to be the "high religious and moral qualities which are the hallmarks of one who is prepared to engage himself in the study which investigates the cause of all existence – the search for the truth which lies behind all human experience" (*Thirtieth Degree*, p. 6).

The candidate for the thirtieth degree "is taught that only by overcoming the fear of death, in lending no credence whatever to superstition and by denying self-interest, can he attain to man's crowning achievement which is the dedication of his life to the Glory of Almighty God and the advancement of His Kingdom among men. This solemn vow of dedication is sealed by an offering of incense upon the altar" (*Thirtieth Degree*, p. 7).

At the conclusion of the thirtieth degree working and having symbolically ascended and descended a ladder representing moral tenets and "the material labours in the study and practice of the Arts and Sciences", the candidate is created a Grand Elect Knight Kadosh, "obligated to eradicate from his own nature the vices of cruelty, fanaticism, superstition and greed". He is exhorted "to equip himself with the qualities demonstrated in the mysterious ladder so that he may be able 'boldly to withstand the evils of fanaticism and superstition, wheresoever and in whatsoever guise they may be found, knowing that the Lord of Truth Himself will be with him in that hour to guide him in all that is true'" (*Thirtieth Degree*, p. 10).

Quoting Ephesians 6:12-18, the Booklet concludes, "Thus armed a Grand Elect Knight Kadosh need fear no enemy of the soul and he may hope, after life's conflict is over, to find a place at the footstool of the Throne on High" (*Thirtieth Degree*, p. 12).

If it had expected to find in the A. & A.S.R. a masonic system where at last the mists of fable had cleared away to reveal a clear and unambiguous allegiance to orthodox Christian doctrine, the Working Party was disappointed. What the members heard and read of the institution rang true to its origin in the deism of the French Enlightenment period. Two facets in particular gave the Working Party cause for concern.

First, it appears that the central facts of the gospel – the incarnation, the cross, the resurrection, Pentecost – are removed from the historical reality emphasised in the creeds of the Church. They are theorised and emasculated so that they fit the masonic system as a mysterious journey towards moral perfection. The impression is that the gospel has been allegorised and reduced to a system of morality, and that the candidate's progress is a travesty of the Christian's relationship in baptism and faith with the once-for-all completed atonement by Christ.

Second, while there are oblique and distorted references to the gospel facts, it appears that it is the candidate himself who journeys from darkness to light, from death-to-self to resurrection, somehow making atonement for himself. This leaves the Working Party suspecting that the so-called "Christian" degrees of Freemasonry are less than aptly named.

APPENDIX II

THE USE OF THE BIBLE IN FREEMASONRY

by Professor Robert Davidson

If it be true that "the Bible plays an important role in Freemasonry; it is the basis of our teaching", as has been claimed, then it is important to look at the ways in which the Bible is used in masonic rituals. It is indeed perhaps one of the attractions of Freemasonry for Christians that so much of its ritual claims to have roots in the Bible, particularly in the traditions concerning Solomon and the Temple. A detailed analysis of the use of biblical material in masonic documents would require a lengthy dissertation. Two things, however, are immediately evident and disturbing.

1   In many cases what masquerades as "biblical" is no more than legend lacking any firm basis in the Bible. To take but one example – Hiram of Tyre is mentioned in I Kings ch. 7 as the master craftsman in bronze who worked on Solomon's Temple. In II Chronicles, ch. 4, v. 16, he is referred to as Huram-Abi. Round this slender base there has grown extensive legendary material concerning Hiram Abiff and his "unshakeable fidelity and noble death". This is supposed to influence the Masons' attitude towards death. There may here be some links with post-biblical Jewish legend which transported Hiram to Paradise as a reward for his work on the Temple, but there is

13

no hint of this in the Bible itself. It is hard to escape the conclusion that the Hiram legend is but a pale parody of the biblical Christian attitude towards death based on the death and resurrection of Jesus. Parody indeed is the word which immediately springs to mind concerning much of the so-called biblical material in masonic documents. How can there be a true use of the biblical material when there is a conspicuous lack of any reference whatsoever in Craft Masonic rituals or in prayers to Jesus Christ, who from the Christian standpoint is the centre of the entire biblical revelation?

2   To those who are unfamiliar with the original languages, the use made of what purports to be Hebrew or other Ancient Near-Eastern words must seem impressive and doubtless the use of Hebrew letters scattered across the documents adds to the sense of mystery. Much of it, however, is linguistic nonsense which anyone with a minimum knowledge of Hebrew can immediately recognise as such. For example, the explanation of the mysterious compound name JA-BUL-ON in Lecture 3 of the Supreme Grand Royal Arch Chapter of Scotland as being the name of God in three (or four) different languages is totally unjustified.

JA is not Chaldean for "I am", nor is it the
Hebrew for "I shall be".

BUL is not the Syriac word for "Lord" or
"Powerful" nor is it a compound word made
up of the preposition "in" or "on" plus
"Heaven" or "On High".

Nor is ON an Egyptian word meaning "Father".

To conclude, therefore, that this name means "I am and shall be Lord in Heaven on High, the Powerful, the Father of all" is wholly misleading. Furthermore, when Hebrew letters are scattered round the divine triangle the explanations given to them are such that their inaccuracy should be evident to anyone with an elementary knowledge of Hebrew.

Over and over again the way in which biblical material is used points to a type of mystery cult or Gnosticism wholly different from faith in the God revealed in the Bible who "did not speak in secret" (Isaiah 45:19), who made known to his people, Israel, his true nature and rightful demands and who in Jesus dwelt "among us full of grace and truth" (John 1:14). Any use of biblical material which conceals these fundamental evangelical insights is unbiblical.

APPENDIX III

ADVICE TO MINISTERS

The existence of Freemasonry within the membership of the Church of Scotland has from time to time presented ministers with difficulty. A minister may know many members to be Freemasons, yet have profound reservations about the craft. She or he may be asked to conduct a service at which a lodge is present, or may be involved with a funeral service where a masonic rite is performed. The minister may suspect subtle pressure to join the order or may feel uneasy about the influence of office-bearers who have a strong tie in another place. Needless to say, such situations are not perceived as problems by ministers who are themselves freemasons.

Ministers, elders and members of the Church of Scotland will nevertheless always remember that their first loyalty is to the Lord Jesus Christ and their highest commitment is to seek the unity and peace of his Church. This primary allegiance on the part of all Christians must be the factor which ensures concord in the worship, mission and fellowship of the Church even where there is a profound disagreement about the nature of Freemasonry and the appropriateness of the Christian's belonging to the order. Only in Christ are the dividing walls broken down and only in Christ is communion with the Father assured for this life and the next.

The following simple guidelines are offered to ministers who are uneasy with the relationship.

In the matter of masonic presence at worship, the lodge will normally observe the courtesy of formally requesting permission to attend. There is no need, unless the minister so wishes, for this to be referred to the Kirk Session. The invitation to worship in a parish church is extended to all and, on balance, it would seem right to assure the lodge that members will be welcome at the normal diet of worship. This is consistent with the advice given to the Panel's Working Party at its meeting with Grand Lodge that there is "no such thing as a 'masonic service'".

At times it has been suggested that a masonic chaplain might conduct worship in a parish church when a lodge is in attendance. It is for the parish minister to decide whether or not to invite a masonic clergyman. Where she or he chooses to do so it will be remembered that, under Presbytery supervision, the parish minister alone is responsible for worship. It is she or he and not a visiting minister who will determine the order and elements of any service.

The wearing of regalia and uniform of various kinds is an issue which arises whenever youth organisations, armed forces, local authority councils and numerous official and voluntary bodies attend a service. Approval of an organisation by the Church cannot be assumed because individual members of that organisation choose to wear its insignia when at worship. In this instance it would be best to leave the matter entirely to the freemasons who attend.

As far as funeral rites are concerned, the minister will understand that, with the blessing, the service is ended. Any masonic ritual which may follow the service is a matter between lodge and family. Cases have arisen where the deceased has had a strong masonic connection and the family has requested that the service be conducted by a masonic chaplain. Care should be taken in this sensitive area to consult fully with the parish minister who cannot insist upon conducting the funeral service but will be involved in pastoral care of the bereaved.

In its contacts with masonic bodies the Working Party has been assured at every stage that Freemasonry considers itself complementary to and supportive of the Church. Many ministers will continue to have grave reservations about the order, considering at the least that the tenets and ritual of the craft are less than worthy of the gospel. Such

16

genuine scruples should not influence the minister's pastoral relationships. Nothing will be gained by alienating men who, by definition, see no inconsistency between their membership of lodge and Church.

The masonic orders are at pains to state that far from threatening the Church they are supportive of it. On its own terms, however, and with reference to the gospel, the Church may usefully care to acknowledge the challenge presented by Freemasonry. Here is an organisation which attracts the loyalty of many men by seeking to fulfil a number of basic human needs. Are these needs being fully met within the Church as we know it? For instance:

1   The need for companionship and a sense of belonging. Is the Church faithfully living as the communion of men and women of every race and age, gathered into Christ?

2   The value and respect of office and role. Does the Church adequately recognise the personal ministry given by Christ to each baptised, so that the body is built up, each member depending upon the other?

3   The importance of ritual and symbolism. Is sufficient care given to the rehearsal of God's mighty acts of salvation in Jesus Christ through the tradition and liturgy of the Church?

There is something amiss if men find these needs met in the lodge and perceive them to be lacking in the Church. Herein lies the challenge then – that the gospel of the love and grace of God in Jesus Christ held out in word and sacrament and in faithful pastoring should eclipse all else by its truth, light and beauty.